To Francis,

Happy Holiday &
a Happy New Year

Cheryl Marie Donaway

THE
CUCINA BELLA
COOKBOOK

Dear Ranny,
Friends make the
best memories.
To our Best Friend
Happy Holidays -
Love YA A whole
crunchy Bunch
Annie Bill
Liam +
Clancy
P.S. No crying!!

THE CUCINA BELLA COOKBOOK
Authentic Italian Comfort Foods

Mark Donaway
& Susan Shafer

Editors
Victor Latino
Kyle Storjohann

Consulting Editors
Todd, Mary, & Sammy Willis
Brenda Willis

Design
Jennifer Gritton
Graphic Design

Photography
Randy Tunnell

Jacket Photography
George Papadakis

Food Stylist
Mark Donaway

Recipe Testing
Susan Shafer

Illustrations
Helen Taylor

Hair & Makeup
Debra Jacobson

Color Separations
Crown Color Corporation

Printing
Impressions Unlimited

Cucina Bella
543 West Diversey Parkway
Chicago, Illinois 60614
773-868-1119

for John Mongaraz, Jeffery Novak,
Kate Koger and Lucy Miller

INTRODUCTION

My first visit to Cucina Bella was as a customer. Being a server myself, I am always intrigued by new restaurants. So when a new one specializing in "Country Italian Comfort Food" appeared in my own neighborhood, I couldn't resist.

Stepping in from Diversey Parkway, a bustling city thoroughfare in the North Lincoln Park area of Chicago, I was immediately seduced by a charming and comfortable calm. This place was beautiful, but refreshingly casual. The walls were filled with family photographs and lined with home-made canned fruits and vegetables. None of the antique chairs matched. The tables were set with mismatched plates and silverware. Food was being served in a variety of interesting bowls, plates, and antique cookware. The overall effect was country and cozy and family. I couldn't remember the last time I felt this comfortable in a restaurant.

And the food! After a first glance at the menu and "Chef's Specialties" list, I was a little baffled, but salivated. I didn't see the usual Italian fare. Instead, flash-fried rice balls called arancini; an "insalata rustica," a salad of spinach, romaine lettuce with peas, corn, strawberries, and grapes in a balsamic dressing with parmesan; a portabella mushroom and spinach lasagna with a mushroom cream sauce; and on and on. I ordered all of the above (much more than I usually eat, but I couldn't help myself).

Well, two weeks later I was working at Cucina Bella. Actually, two weeks later I was adopted into the Cucina Bella "family," and it truly is a family. My first day there I met the owner and principal chef, Mark Donaway, his mother, Brenda Willis, a successful professional who enjoys coming in to hostess whenever she can, and his grandmother, "Nana" Koger, who came in from northern Indiana to deliver more of her canned fruits (I soon found myself calling her "Nana," like everyone else in the "family").

The sous chefs, Susan Shafer and Charlie Socher, had been with Mark for years. Susan started with Mark in his first restaurant, Eughie's (in Homewood, Ill.), seven years before, and Charlie had joined the family with Donaways, An American Cafe a couple of years before.

Like myself, the small service staff, the "children" of Cucina Bella, is composed primarily of "trainers" from corporate restaurant chains who got tired of the "sales grind." Others have come and gone, for one reason or another, but the faithful remain to befriend and serve the neighborhood. Most important, all remain welcome members of the family.

So, from the blood, sweat, tears, and love of "our family," what you are holding is a collection of recipes that any Italian grandmother would be proud to serve her family and that can also be prepared by absolutely ANYONE!

Mange! Ciao Bella!   Richard Roberts

FOREWORD

Some wished us luck. Others said it couldn't be done, especially in a city the size of Chicago. But, as we readied to open the doors to the first customers of Cucina Bella, we proudly surveyed the restaurant, knowing we had accomplished what was most important: we were standing in a comfortable, rustic space that could be an extension of your own home. Somewhere to go for a wonderful, hearty, back-to-the-basics meal while blanketed by the feeling of having never left your grandmother's.

It was at that moment we realized that this was not the end result of the labors of a group of strangers. We set out to create a restaurant and had ended up with a family. Some were intentional choices; others were unexpected miracles. How they got here became unimportant, for now they were as much a part of Cucina Bella as we.

As the staff came together in the kitchen, prior to the ceremonial unlocking of the front door, we were hit by the overwhelming feeling that this was the heart and soul of Cucina Bella. Of any family, really. Everyone gathered in the kitchen — sharing. Try as we might, could we bring that very special feeling to each table? We were confident we could. Remembering the words "better safe than sorry," we added our Kitchen Table. Yes, a table smack dab in the middle of the kitchen!

Those feelings, so strongly felt by us, must have been contagious, because soon after, the kitchen table was booked solid up to six months in advance. Every night we proudly watched from behind the line as our guests laughed, loved, and shared in our home. Then something happened we never expected. People started asking for a cookbook. They actually wanted to take a part of Cucina Bella home with them!

We looked to each other, asking did we have it in us?! The question then became, how could we not? Our menu offers the comfort that had been passed down from generations of our families. We felt an obligation to "pass down" as well.

Who knew such a simple question would set into motion rigorous planning meetings, phone calls, more meetings, faxes, long photo shoots, botched photo shoots, illustrations, reshoots, copyright and scantron applications, and nine drafts of the cookbook? Not to mention the testing. Over a period of many months, loyal customers, friends, and family tested the recipes. They were told to be keenly aware of not only taste but time and preparation. If it wasn't simple, what good would it be to you?

The recipes that follow are the fruition of all the hard work of those many months. A simple thank you to all those who helped seems hardly enough. We are eternally grateful to everyone.

So, from our family to yours . . .

Paul & Nancy Susan Shafer

"With the publication of this beautifully written and photographed book, the 'secret' of Cucina Bella's great success is out — there is no great secret! What is revealed in these inviting recipes is that Chef Mark Donaway and his colleague Susan Shafer have the courage to remain true to the basics of great Italian home cooking. Simplicity is at the heart of all true genius and anyone who has ever been pleasured by the cooking at Cucina Bella knows he or she is in the hands of master chefs. Eating Cucina Bella food, either at the restaurant or from dishes prepared from these recipes, is a guarantee of what we seek most in life — warmth, comfort, and love. In other words, Cucina Bella food makes us feel very deeply and wonderfully at home."

John Callaway

John D. Callaway is the host of Chicago Tonight
on WTTW, PBS in Chicago and author of the
best-selling book of essays "The Thing of It Is."
Chicago, Illinois

"Forget Prozac. Forget therapy. If you want to feel that life is good, go to Cucina Bella. What makes it a great restaurant is that they are able to satisfy three major human needs; they fill your stomachs, they fill your senses, and because they care so much, they fill your heart. ...What more could you ask for? Okay — the love of your life — but that's been known to be found there, too."

Ann Hampton Callaway

Singer-composer
Croton-on-Hudson, New York

"Ditto"

Liz Callaway

Singer-Broadway star
New York, New York

"Chef/Restaurateur Mark Donaway and Chef Sue Shafer are two of the most tasty chefs around. Their presentation is excellent and their creativity most unique...taste and presentation...unlike any restaurant I've visited in the States. The Chef's table is perhaps the most romantic table in Chicago...the kitchen table experience is a stroke of culinary genius... the outdoor street cafe will excite your senses...I can't wait to start using the recipes..."

Cindy Kurman
Kurman Communications
Chicago, Illinois

"The best authentic carbonara I've ever put to my lips!"

Dave Edwards
Chicago, Illinois

"Cucina Bella is homestyle Italian, tantalizing, aromatic, every taste reminiscent of Italy!"

Kim Walton & Phil Buckman
Chicago, Illinois

"...everything was perfect. A true delight. Thank you and congratulations on the best restaurant in Chicago."

The Haramaras
Chicago, Illinois

"The Romans thought that they knew what a food orgy was — well they can't hold a candle to you!"

Bill Fisher
Las Vegas, Nevada

Friendship Chicken, page 87

Cucina Bella Dining Room

CONTENTS

Appetizers

ARANCINI
(Fried Rice Balls)

Our favorite "holiday food" is popular for seasonal gatherings, birthdays and anniversaries. Serve them hot with warm marinara. Finish with grated Parmesan. Crusty Italian bread to sop up the sauce is perfect.

1 cup rice
1 tablespoon dried oregano
1 tablespoon dried basil
1 tablespoon olive oil
2 cups water

In a covered pan boil the above ingredients for 13 minutes, or until rice is done and water has evaporated. Spread rice mixture on cookie sheet to cool. Put mixture in large mixing bowl. Add

1/4 cup grated provolone
1/3 cup sweet peas
1/2 teaspoon salt
1/2 teaspoon pepper

Combine mixture and make 2-inch balls, firmly packed, like a snowball. To bread:

1/4 cup flour
3 beaten eggs
2 cups breadcrumbs
3 cups vegetable oil (for frying)

Roll the arancini first in flour, then into egg mixture and lastly in the breadcrumbs. Preheat frying oil to 375 degrees. Fry arancini in small batches for 1 1/2 minutes or until golden brown.

Serves 6 to 8

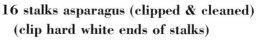

GRILLED ASPARAGUS

A great summer starter that can be served hot or cold. A perfect companion to Cucina Bella Corn Polenta.

16 stalks asparagus (clipped & cleaned)
 (clip hard white ends of stalks)
1 lemon (sliced in half)
5 oz olive oil (put in medium mixing bowl)
4 oz Gorgonzola cheese

Squeeze 1/2 lemon with olive oil in medium mixing bowl. Add asparagus and marinate for 15 minutes. On a hot grill, cook asparagus for 1 minute on each side. Place on large plate. Sprinkle with crumbled Gorgonzola cheese and the juice from the remaining lemon. Salt and pepper to taste.

Serves 4 to 6

Baked Garlic is one of Cucina Bella's most requested recipes and favorite starter. Serve with crusty Italian bread or our favorite bruschette croutons.

6 bulbs jumbo elephant garlic
1 sprig rosemary
4 tablespoons olive oil
3 cups hot water

Place all ingredients in a baking pan or oven-proof casserole and cover with aluminum foil. (Rosemary leaves should be detached.) Bake in oven at 450 degrees for 45 minutes. Garlic should be soft to the touch. Drain on paper towel or kitchen towel and slice tops of garlic off, exposing the meat (soft) inside. Serve hot. Drizzle olive oil on tops of garlic. This will keep them from drying out on top.

Serves 4 to 6

TRADITIONAL ANTIPASTO

Arrange on a large plate, making a pretty pattern. Serve with Italian bread, butter & olive oil. This great starter is a perfect substitute for a salad course.

4 thin slices salami
4 thin slices prosciutto
4 anchovy filets
2 celery stalks (cut in half)
8 large green olives
2 teaspoons capers
4 artichoke hearts in olive oil
1 small jar pimentos
4 slices tomato
4 vinegar peppers
8 black ripe olives

Serves 2 to 4

VENETIAN STYLE OYSTERS

8 fresh raw oysters
2 teaspoons lemon juice
dash cayenne pepper
2 teaspoons caviar

Open oysters, saving both shells. Mix lemon juice, cayenne and caviar and spread thinly over each oyster. Close shells and serve on ice or rock salt.

Serves 2 to 4

PROSCIUTTO WITH CANTALOUPE & MELON

This simple starter is as easy as it is a tradition.

Chill cantaloupe & melon, and cut each into 4 to 8 slices. Remove seeds and rinds. Wrap with pieces of prosciutto. Serve chilled.

1 small cantaloupe
1 small melon
1/2 pound prosciutto (sliced thin)

Serves 6 to 8

FIGS & PROSCIUTTO

When fresh figs are in season, this easy recipe will impress even the most discriminating palate.

4 to 8 figs* (fresh)
1/2 pound prosciutto (sliced thin)

Chill figs and wrap each with prosciutto. Serve with Caper Relish and a light drizzle of olive oil.

*Dates can be substituted for figs. Remove pits and grill for 20 seconds

The natural sugar from the dates will help hold the prosciutto in place.

Serves 6 to 8

FRIED MOZZARELLA & PROVOLONE

Provolone cheese is sharp and full bodied, which adds a wonderful unexpected taste to this simple standard.

2 eggs of fresh mozzarella (quartered)
1 lb fresh provolone (cut into 16 cubes)
1 cup flour (in small bowl)
4 cups frying oil (in pan at 375 degrees)
3 eggs whipped (in small bowl)
1/4 teaspoon salt
2 cups breadcrumbs

Roll cheeses in salted flour, dip in egg and roll in breadcrumbs. Fry in oil for 1 minute or until golden brown. Drain on paper towel or kitchen towel. Serve hot with Cucina Bella Marinara or Sun-Dried Tomato Relish.

Serves 4 to 6

Herbed Oven-Browned Potatoes, page 29

SUN-DRIED TOMATO RELISH

In a mixing bowl combine all ingredients; salt and pepper to taste. Serve chilled or at room temperature with Italian bread, fried cheese or almost any Cucina Bella starter.

8 oz sliced sun-dried tomatoes (soak in hot water for 20 minutes to reconstitute, discard water)

2 oz fresh chopped basil

2 oz pine nuts (toasted in oven at 350 degrees for 5 minutes)

3 oz olive oil

1 oz balsamic vinegar

Serves 4 to 6

CAPER RELISH

Combine all ingredients in mixing bowl; salt and pepper to taste. Serve cold or at room temperature with Italian bread or your favorite starter. Be creative.

8 oz capers (drained)
2/3 cup walnuts (toasted in oven at
    350 degrees for 5 minutes)
1 garlic clove (minced)
4 oz sweet peas
2 tablespoons olive oil
1/4 cup fresh diced basil

Serves 4 to 6

BRUSCHETTE

(Italian Garlic Bread)

As simple as it can be. But, oh what a way to start a meal.

1 loaf crusty Italian bread (sliced into
1/2-inch-thick slices — lengthwise)
4 fresh garlic cloves (minced)
4 oz olive oil
salt

Drizzle olive oil on each slice of bread. Rub each slice with garlic. Sprinkle with salt. Bake in oven at 400 degrees for 5 minutes until golden brown. Easy variations on this recipe: simply add chopped tomatoes & basil. Rub with pesto. Add toasted walnuts & fresh pear (toast walnuts in oven at 350 degrees for 3 minutes) or our favorite, chopped tomatoes, Gorgonzola & Parmesan cheese. Bruschette can also make delicious garlic croutons. Just cube a slice of Bruschette.

Serves 6 to 8

TUSCAN BEAN SALAD

This traditional starter is a perfect choice for a dinner party or a quick choice to impress that special someone at a romantic dinner for two.

1 1/2 cups white beans (soak 24 hours, keep in water and refrigerate)
6 whole cloves garlic (chopped)
1 tablespoon rosemary
1/2 tablespoon dried oregano
1/2 tablespoon dried basil
8 oz marinara
1 tablespoon lemon juice
salt & pepper to taste

In a medium pot add water to cover the beans. Add garlic, rosemary, oregano and basil. Cook for 50 minutes. Beans should be tender. Pour off any remaining water. Cool mixture. Add lemon juice and marinara. Salt & pepper to taste. Serve cold.

Serves 4 to 6

TUSCAN BEAN SPREAD

Follow the same directions as above. When you pour off water to cool, transfer beans to food processor. Add lemon juice, marinara, salt & pepper. Serve with crusty Italian bread and olive oil.

Serves 4 to 6

POMODORINI GRATINATI
(Baked Stuffed Tomatoes)

This popular menu item still remains a Cucina Bella favorite. The key is fresh ingredients and preparation just before serving.

4 large tomatoes (hollowed out)
9 oz breadcrumbs
1 tablespoon Parmesan cheese
2 cloves garlic (minced)
2 tablespoons olive oil
1 teaspoon dried oregano
1 teaspoon dried basil
1 tablespoon Worcestershire sauce
1/2 cup sweet peas

In a bowl mix all ingredients and stuff tomatoes; salt and pepper to taste. Bake at 350 degrees for 15 minutes. Tomatoes should be soft. Serve on a bed of Tuscan Bean Salad. Finish with fresh shaved Parmesan cheese.

Serves 4

MINESTRONE RUSTICA

(Rustic Vegetable Soup)

This hearty recipe is a staple at Cucina Bella. We modify our version to accommodate our vegetarian clients. This is the original version, perfect for parties and cold winter nights. Bread for sopping is essential.

1/2 lb Italian sausage
1 lb spareribs
1/2 medium cabbage (shredded)
1 cup corn
1 cup sweet peas
2 stalks celery (diced)
2 medium onions (sliced)
1/2 teaspoon each of salt & pepper
2 teaspoons chopped parsley
1/2 teaspoon dried oregano
1/2 teaspoon dried basil
1/2 teaspoon diced garlic
2 carrots (diced)
2 zucchini (diced)
3 potatoes (diced)
1 1/2 cups white beans (soak 24 hours
  in water, keep refrigerated)

Mix all vegetables together, divide in half and place one half in large soup pan. Add enough water to cover vegetables. Add salt and pepper, herbs and beans. Place sausage and spareribs on vegetables. Cover with remaining vegetables. Simmer for 3 hours, stirring every 1/2 hour.

Serves 6 to 10

MARINARA RUSTICA
(Cucina Bella Tomato Sauce)

Our rustic marinara is a staple at Cucina Bella, used as a mother sauce for many recipes. Vegetarians rave as well as our truly Italian restaurant fans. We suggest making a whole pot and freezing half to use for other recipes that appear in the Cucina Bella Cookbook.

3 tablespoons olive oil
1 stalk celery (finely chopped)
1 onion (chopped)
1 teaspoon parsley (minced)
1 clove garlic (minced)
1 large can tomatoes
1 carrot (minced, use food processor)
1/2 cup balsamic vinegar
1 medium can tomato puree
1/2 teaspoon salt
1/2 teaspoon pepper
1/2 teaspoon basil (diced)
1/2 teaspoon oregano (diced)

Place oil, celery, onion, parsley, minced carrot and garlic in medium-to-large pot and brown lightly. Add balsamic vinegar, tomatoes, tomato puree. Salt and pepper and simmer for 45 minutes. Stir every 15 minutes. Add basil and oregano and cook for 10 more minutes. 1/2 pound butter (unsalted) can be substituted for the olive oil if preferred. 2 cups water will help thin the sauce if desired.

Serves 6 to 8

HERBED OVEN-
BROWNED POTATOES

We use this recipe as a side for many of our hearty main courses, especially for family-style party menus.

8 potatoes (quartered, skin on)
10 cloves garlic
6 tablespoons olive oil
1/2 teaspoon oregano
2 tablespoons rosemary
1/4 teaspoon salt
dash of red pepper flakes
1/2 tablespoon paprika

Preheat oven at 425 degrees. Put potatoes in bowl. In a food processor, combine garlic, olive oil, salt and herbs. Pour over potatoes, mix and spread out on an aluminum-foil-lined baking pan. Bake for 30 minutes. Turn potatoes and bake for 15 additional minutes.

Serves 6 to 10

See photograph on page 18

GARLIC MASHED POTATOES

This homey, simple recipe is the perfect side for any meal. Grilled portabella mushrooms have proven to be a perfect marriage.

8 potatoes (diced with skin on)
1 tablespoon salt

Add potatoes and salt to a pot of water and boil for 30 minutes. Potatoes should be tender. Pour off water and mash potatoes with potato masher or large fork. Add the following ingredients

4 tablespoons butter
salt and pepper to taste
1/2 cup hot milk
1 1/2 tablespoons minced garlic

Beat potatoes with an electric mixer until potatoes are creamy. To help fluff the potatoes, cover the pot and place over a low flame for 5 minutes.

Serves 6 to 8

CUCINA BELLA MEATBALLS

The popularity of our meatballs has always astounded us but only proves that traditional cooking is what the general public craves. We use this recipe with our marinara sauce and the obvious spaghetti. Cucina Bella Meatballs are also a perfect starter or side for a main course.

1/2 lb chopped beef
1/2 lb chopped veal
1/2 lb chopped pork
1 clove garlic (minced)
2 tablespoons chopped Italian parsley
salt and pepper to taste
1/2 cup breadcrumbs
1/4 cup milk
2 eggs (lightly beaten)
1/3 cup grated Parmesan

Preheat oven at 325 degrees. Combine all ingredients. Mix thoroughly and shape into 12 balls or 24 smaller ones. Bake in oven at 350 degrees for 25 minutes or until cooked thoroughly and brown on the outside. Cooking time may vary because of size of meatballs.

Serves 4 to 8

See photograph on page 68

CUCINA BELLA CORN POLENTA

Serve corn polenta as an appetizer or an incredible authentic side for a main course.

2 cups cornmeal
1 cup corn (fresh off the cob or frozen)
3 tablespoons olive oil
2 teaspoons salt
1/2 stick unsalted butter
   (room temperature for 1 hour)

In a cooking pot boil 9 cups water. Add olive oil & salt. Carefully add cornmeal, stirring constantly. On a low heat continue to stir for 5 minutes. Add butter and corn. Continue to cook until butter has melted. Polenta should be thick and creamy.

Serves 6

POTATO PARSLEY GNOCCHI

Potato Parsley Gnocchi are one of our favorites but are time-consuming to produce. The payoff is certainly worth it, as you will find out. Serve with Cucina Bella Marinara or Panna sauce.

3 large potatoes (diced, skin-on, boil in water approx. 20 minutes, then mash with potato masher)
2 cups flour
2 eggs
1/2 cup chopped Italian parsley
3 tablespoons melted butter
2 oz grated Parmesan cheese
salt & pepper to taste

In a large mixing bowl mix mashed potatoes, flour, eggs, parsley, salt & pepper, 2 tablespoons melted butter and knead into a dough. Shape dough into 1/2 inch rolls. Cut into 1-inch pieces and form into crescent shape. Cook crescents in boiling salted water for 4 minutes. Remove, using a slotted spoon. Sprinkle with Parmesan cheese and 1 tablespoon melted butter. Serve with your favorite sauce.

Serves 6 to 8

SALADS

INSALATA CIAO BELLA

(Hello Beautiful House Salad)

The name says it all. This crisp, light house salad has been with us for a long time. Perfect for any occasion.

1/2 red onion (sliced and separated into rings)
1 tomato (sliced into eight pieces)
1 head fresh romaine lettuce (rinsed & cleaned)
1/2 cup olive oil (extra virgin)
1/4 cup balsamic vinegar
pinch of salt & pepper

In a chilled mixing bowl combine all ingredients and mix thoroughly. Salt and pepper to taste. Serve in chilled salad bowls, arranging onions and tomatoes on top.

Serves 6 to 8

Mushroom Walnut Gorgonzola Salad

This simple salad recipe has appeared on four menus for the past ten years. Its popularity has been amazing. The Italian motto "Less is more" or "Let the quality of the food speak for itself" applies perfectly to this favorite salad (nicknamed "GorgMush").

2 cups crumbled Gorgonzola cheese
   (Italian blue cheese)
3/4 cup walnuts (roast in oven for
   5 minutes at 350 degrees)
1 1/2 cups quartered button mushrooms
1/4 cup olive oil

In a chilled mixing bowl combine all ingredients; salt and pepper to taste. Serve in chilled salad bowls with lettuce garnish.

Serves 6 to 8

CAESAR SALAD

Our version of this ever-popular salad is our favorite as well as our employees' and my mother's. We use no cream, mayonnaise or excess fats like most caesar recipes. Instead, our version relies on family secrets & traditional approaches. Caesar dressing is one of our most requested recipes.

4 anchovy filets
1 1/2 teaspoon garlic
2 oz Worcestershire sauce
2 oz balsamic vinegar
6 oz olive oil
1 oz Parmesan cheese
3 pinches salt
1 pinch pepper
2 egg yolks
1 head romaine (rinsed & cleaned)

In a food processor blend all ingredients. In a large mixing bowl mix blended ingredients with romaine lettuce. Serve in chilled salad bowls and garnish with fresh shaved Parmesan cheese and garlic croutons.

Serves 4 to 6

INSALATA RUSTICA
(Rustic Mixed Greens Salad)

A simple mixed greens salad was often requested, which prompted Sue and me to develop this rustic version. Dandelion greens were the perfect addition, but they sometimes are difficult to locate. Do not fret, any substitutions will work. Do not pick out of your back yard!

2 oz chopped radicchio
4 oz spinach
6 oz dandelion greens
6 oz romaine lettuce
1/2 cup grapes
3 sliced strawberries
1 oz balsamic vinegar
2 oz olive oil
2 oz grated Parmesan cheese
1/2 grilled onion
salt & pepper to taste

Brush onion with olive oil and grill. Chill. In mixing bowl combine remaining ingredients. Toss gently. Finish with chilled grilled onions on top.

Serves 4 to 6

GRILLED SQUID SALAD

This recipe was one of our favorites during our travels to Italy. The fresh squid of Italy's fishing regions are second to none and perfect for fast grilling.

3 lb. squid cleaned & cut (cut after grilling)
1 cup olive oil (extra virgin)
1 stalk celery (finely diced)
1/2 cup lemon juice
1 teaspoon diced fresh garlic
1 pinch red pepper flakes
1/2 cup chopped fresh basil
1/2 cup chopped fresh parsley
salt & pepper to taste

Grill whole calamari (approx. 1 minute). Set to cool. Cut calamari into rings. Cut tentacles in 2 pieces each (in half). Combine all ingredients in chilled mixing bowl. Chill for one hour. Re-toss and serve on chilled plates with lettuce or fresh herb garnish.

GRILLED ONION SALAD WITH SHAVED PARMESAN

This simple salad screams summer cookout specialty. Try to say that five times fast. Remember that fresh mint is key to this recipe. We developed this one for our summer outdoor street café menu.

3 large yellow or red onions
9 tablespoons virgin olive oil
1/2 teaspoon salt
1/2 teaspoon pepper
1/2 cup fresh Italian parsley
1/4 cup fresh diced lemon mint
1 fresh lemon or 1/4 cup lemon juice
4 oz grated fresh Parmesan cheese

Trim ends of onions, peel and cut horizontally into 5/8-inch slices. Brush them with olive oil and sprinkle with salt and pepper. Grill onions 6 - 10 minutes a side. Outside should be charred and inside cooked soft. Let cool. In chilled salad bowl separate onions into rings and combine with remaining ingredients. With a vegetable peeler shave fresh Parmesan on top. Chill and serve.

Serves 6 to 8

See photograph on page 59

PANZANELLA
(Italian Bread Salad)

This recipe was originally created as a way to make use of old, stale bread. Creative Tuscans softened the old bread with water to create this simple thrifty salad. To stay with a theme, serve with Peasants Pasta for a festival of leftovers.

1/2 loaf cubed, dried bread (soak in water for 30 seconds just before you begin to assemble salad)
1 head chopped romaine lettuce
1 large tomato (chopped)
1 onion (chopped)
2 cloves garlic (diced)
1/2 cup diced fresh basil
2/3 cup olive oil
1/3 cup balsamic vinegar
salt & pepper to taste

Combine all ingredients in chilled mixing bowl. Salt and pepper to taste. Serve in chilled salad bowls and garnish with fresh grated Parmesan.

Serves 6 to 8

INSALATA CAPRESE
(Grilled Salami & Eggplant Salad)

This recipe is a great expansion of an Italian classic. Fresh basil and fresh mozzarella are key to its success. Serve hot or cold.

8 slices eggplant (1/4 inch thick)
8 slices salami (1/4 inch thick)
8 slices mozzarella
1 oz olive oil
1 stalk fresh basil (diced finely)
pinch of dried oregano
1 stalk fresh basil for garnish
salt & pepper to taste

Rub eggplant slices with olive oil and sprinkle with salt, pepper & dried oregano. Grill salami & eggplant for 1 minute on each side. On a large plate, place a piece of eggplant, mozzarella and salami overlapping each other. Continue process until you have used all ingredients. Sprinkle with salt & pepper, diced basil and olive oil. Garnish with fresh basil.

Serves 6 to 8

FONTINA SALAD

Fontina cheese is the gem of Northern Italy and is made from the milk of Alpine cattle. Similar cheeses made elsewhere are called fontal. The peasant style salad is perfect with fontina cubed or crumbled. Fresh mint leaves make a great aromatic garnish. Fontina cheese is a great table cheese and goes well with fruit; hence this inspired recipe.

8 oz fontina cheese (cubed or crumbled)
1 apple (cored & diced) (store in 1 cup lemon juice to keep fruit from browning)
1 pear (cored & diced) (store in 1 cup lemon juice to keep fruit from browning)
4 oz pecans (toasted 5 minutes in oven at 350 degrees)
2 oz olive oil
1 oz balsamic vinegar
1/2 lemon

In a large mixing bowl combine all ingredients and chill for 30 minutes. Do not include lemon juice from fruit. Serve on chilled plates or elegant stemware with lettuce and fresh mint garnish.

Serves 4 to 6

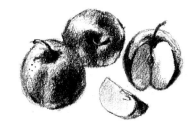

Uncle's Finger Salad

Sue's half brother, Bob (a great cook), had an Uncle Don (a master chef), who invented this simple salad. Uncle Don is now dead. They say that 40 days after his burial, seven garlic plants spontaneously emerged from the soil over the very spot where he was laid to rest. Uncle's Finger Salad is very garlicky, very Italian and very wonderful.

1 head romaine lettuce (cleaned and detached)
4 cloves garlic (minced in food processor)
1 cup olive oil (add to minced garlic in food processor)
1/3 cup fresh grated Romano cheese
1/2 cup fresh grated Parmesan cheese
2 tablespoons red wine vinegar
Fresh cracked peppercorns (a mixture of black, red, green and white)

Combine all ingredients in a chilled mixing bowl. The amount of fresh cracked peppercorns is to taste. Lots is the best idea. Serve with homemade croutons or crusty Italian bread. Salad should be eaten with your fingers.

Serves 6 to 8

Pasta

PAESANA

If this recipe is not the perfect example of Italian comfort foods, I'll eat my hat! Well...I'll just eat the Paesana, my favorite dish on the menu.

24 oz Cucina Bella Marinara
10 oz precooked Italian sausage (cooked in 10 oz of water — save for stock)
1 tablespoon olive oil
5 oz diced mushrooms
5 oz frozen sweet peas
5 oz sausage stock

Sauté mushrooms in olive oil. Add the rest of the ingredients and heat for 10 minutes. Serve with your favorite pasta.

Serves 4 to 6

PUTTANESCA

The origin of this recipe is the ladies of the night, who needed a quick meal while they were working. Puttanesca still remains the most popular pasta at Cucina Bella. Add minced anchovy filets as an option.

24 oz Cucina Bella Marinara
1/2 teaspoon serrano chili paste*
  or 2 to 3 pinches of red chili flakes
3 oz capers
8 oz pitted black olives

In a large pan heat all ingredients. Toss with your favorite pasta. We suggest penne.

*available in Asian markets & specialty food stores

Serves 4 to 6

PESCATORE

Sue and I pride ourselves for our extensive use of fresh seafood. This recipe at Cucina Bella changes constantly due to our commitment to always serve seafood that is top quality.

20 oz Cucina Bella Marinara
1 tablespoon lemon juice
2 pinches red chili flakes
3 oz water
10-12 fresh mussels (cleaned and unopened)
3-5 oz fresh cleaned calamari
3-5 oz fresh scallops

In a large pan heat marinara, lemon juice, water, chilies and mussels. When mussels begin to open (approx. 1 to 3 minutes), add calamari and scallops. Cook for 1 additional minute. Serve with your favorite pasta. We suggest fussilli.

Serves 4 to 6

PRIMAVERA

*During the hot
summer months this
recipe is altered to
a simple garlic herb
oil replacing the
marinara. A lighter
approach has proved
to be most successful.*

2 tablespoons olive oil
2 oz sliced zucchini
1 oz sliced carrot
2 oz diced mushrooms
2 plum tomatoes (quartered)
3 oz corn
3 oz sweet peas
3 oz fresh spinach
salt & pepper to taste
Pinch of red chili flakes
20 oz Cucina Bella Marinara
3 oz water

In a large sauté pan, heat olive oil. In this order, add zucchini, carrot, mushrooms, tomatoes, corn, peas and fresh spinach on top. Salt and pepper to taste. Cook for approximately 2 minutes and then flip or mix vegetables to cook evenly. Add a pinch of chilies, marinara and water. Cook until sauce reduces. Serve this vegetarian delight with spaghetti.

Serves 6 to 8

FUNGHI FUNGHI

The Funghi recipe is the most requested of all of our recipes. The origins of Italian cooking are Greek, Roman, Byzantine and a dash of the Orient. We developed this recipe with the dash of the Orient in mind, as well as our extensive background as pioneers of fusion cuisine. Hence we reveal our secret: mushroom soy sauce (available in most Asian markets or specialty food stores).

2 tablespoons olive oil
3 oz diced shiitake mushrooms
1 oz diced porcini mushrooms
3 oz diced portabella mushrooms
2 tablespoons unsalted butter
10 oz heavy whipping cream
2 tablespoons mushroom soy sauce
salt & pepper to taste

In a large pan add olive oil and cook mushrooms for 2 minutes. Add butter and melt. Add cream, mushroom soy sauce, and salt and pepper to taste. Reduce sauce, stirring occasionally. Serve with your favorite pasta, we suggest penne, and toss with Parmesan cheese before serving.

Serves 4 to 6

PANNA

Cucina Bella's simple white cheese cream sauce, just like Nonna used to make!

12 oz heavy whipping cream
1 tablespoon lemon juice
8 oz grated Parmesan cheese
2 oz grated Romano cheese
1 oz unsalted butter
salt & pepper to taste

In a medium pan heat lemon juice and reduce by half. Add butter and melt. Add whipping cream and reduce. When sauce thickens, add cheeses and whisk thoroughly. Serve with your favorite pasta. We suggest rigatoni, our favorite pasta.

Serves 4

Grilled Onion Salad with Shaved Parmesan, page 42

TRADITIONAL PESTO

Use as a spread for Bruschetta or as a pasta sauce.

2 cups basil
3 tablespoons pine nuts
3 garlic cloves
3 tablespoons Parmesan cheese
1/2 cup olive oil
salt & pepper to taste

In a food processor, combine the ingredients listed above. For pasta sauce, add 1 cup water and reduce. Continue to stir with wooden spoon to keep cheese from sticking. For a cream sauce use 1 cup heavy whipping cream.

Serves 4 to 6

PARSLEY WALNUT PESTO

16 oz Italian parsley (cleaned leaves only)
3 garlic cloves
3 oz walnuts
3 oz olive oil
3 tablespoons Parmesan cheese
salt and pepper to taste
16 oz heavy whipping cream
1 oz butter (unsalted)

In a food processor, combine parsley, walnuts, garlic, olive oil and salt & pepper to taste. Transfer to large cooking pan. Add cream, butter and cheese. Reduce sauce. Toss with your favorite pasta. We suggest rigatoni.

Serves 4 to 6

GORGONZOLA WALNUT CREAM

We love this recipe because of its simplicity and natural layered flavors.

8 oz crumbled Gorgonzola (Italian blue cheese)
6 oz walnuts (toasted 5 minutes
  in oven at 375 degrees)
2 tablespoons Parmesan cheese
1 oz Romano cheese
16 oz heavy whipping cream
salt & pepper to taste

In a large pan combine ingredients and reduce until sauce thickens. Use a wooden spoon to break up pieces of Gorgonzola. Serve over your favorite pasta; we suggest rotini.

Serves 4 to 6

NEAPOLITANA

This simple recipe is derived from the "Working Italian Family." A quick delicious meal to feed the whole family after a hard day's work.

2 cups pitted black olives
   (ground in food processor)
5 cloves crushed garlic
3 plum tomatoes (quartered lengthwise)
1 teaspoon salt
1 oz olive oil
8 oz water
10-15 whole black olives (pitted)
black pepper to taste
1/4 cup grated Romano cheese

Place all ingredients except cheese in large pan. Cook for 7-10 minutes. Toss with spaghetti and cheese.

Serves 4 to 6

NORCINA

The natural combination of sausage and fennel in a cream sauce is an Italian gem of a meal. This recipe often appears on our chef's specialty daily menu.

1 oz olive oil
1 oz unsalted butter
8 oz chopped fennel (fine)
5 oz Italian sausage (precook 10 minutes, drain well and crumble)
1 oz chopped basil
3 oz Parmesan cheese
pinch of dried oregano
1 diced garlic clove
salt & pepper to taste
12 oz heavy whipping cream

In a large pan heat olive oil and cook fennel and sausage. Sausage should be thoroughly cooked; fennel should become transparent and brown. Add remaining ingredients. Reduce. When sauce thickens, serve with penne pasta.

Serves 4 to 6

Portabella Mushroom Lasagna, page 81

TOSCANA

Inspired by extensive research and travel, this incredible recipe will definitely make you a star in your own kitchen.

1/2 white onion (cut into thin rings & separate)
4 oz diced portabella mushrooms
3 oz diced shiitake mushrooms
3 oz diced button mushrooms
pinch of dried basil & oregano
6 oz water
4 oz marinara
1 diced garlic clove
1 oz fresh chopped basil
1/2 tablespoon mushroom soy sauce
1 oz olive oil
salt & pepper to taste

In a large pan heat olive oil and cook onions and mushrooms. (Onions will become transparent and begin to brown.) Add remaining ingredients and reduce. Serve with linguini.

Serves 4 to 6

Cucina Bella Meatballs, page 31

TOSCA

Weight-conscious Chicago divas have begged for this recipe for years. Recipe testers discovered why: it's simple and absolutely delicious.

1 whole white onion
  (cut into thin rings and separate)
1 thinly diced red pepper
  (remove stem and seeds inside; discard)
6 oz water
1 diced garlic clove
4 oz marinara
3 tablespoons chopped fresh basil
1 tablespoon mushroom soy sauce
1 oz olive oil
salt & pepper to taste

In a large pan heat olive oil and brown onions and peppers (onions should be transparent). Add remaining ingredients and reduce. Serve with fettucini.

Serves 4 to 6

PEASANTS PASTA

The Peasants Pasta recipe is based on an Italian custom to make use of all the leftovers at the end of the week.

12 oz heavy whipping cream
1 oz minced garlic
4 oz Parmesan cheese
1 oz unsalted butter
1 tablespoon dried oregano
1/2 tablespoon diced fresh basil
7 oz diced precooked ham
5 oz sweet peas
5 oz corn
1 oz olive oil
salt & pepper to taste

In a pan combine all ingredients. Reduce, stirring occasionally with a wooden spoon. Serve with penne pasta.

Serves 4 to 6

MARGHERITA

This simple recipe is a dieter's dream, or perfect for those who are simply watching their weight. Garlic can be easily deleted. Margherita is a popular summer pasta dish following a hard workout, or for those who are trying to beat the heat of a Chicago summer in our outdoor street café.

10 oz sun-dried tomatoes (diced)
  (soak 24 hours, save sun-dried tomato juice)
4 cloves minced garlic
16 oz sun-dried tomato juice
5 oz diced fresh basil
2 oz olive oil
salt & pepper to taste

Combine all ingredients in large pan and reduce by two-thirds over medium heat. Serve with fettuccini.

Serves 4 to 6

DIAVOLA

*This "hot devil"
pasta has always
been a favorite for
those who live on
the spicy side.*

12 oz heavy whipping cream
1 oz unsalted butter
4 oz Romano cheese
3 cloves minced garlic
salt & pepper to taste
4 oz pecans (toasted 5 minutes
   in oven at 375 degrees)
1 tablespoon diced fresh basil
1/2 teaspoon crushed red chilies
2 oz marinara

In a large pan combine all ingredients and reduce,
stirring occasionally with a wooden spoon. Serve
with buccatini.

Serves 4 to 6

CARUSO

This recipe has literally developed itself over the past 10 years. Salt and pepper are key to the success of this dish.

10 oz chicken livers
1 cup flour, 1 oz dried oregano, 1 oz dried basil (mix in medium mixing bowl)
1 oz olive oil
2 diced tomatoes
2 oz fresh diced basil
1 oz lemon juice
6 oz chicken stock or water
salt & pepper to taste
3 cloves minced garlic
2 tablespoons unsalted butter
1/4 teaspoon dried sage

Drain chicken livers on a paper towel or kitchen towel and dredge them in bowl of flour and herbs. Set aside. In a large pan heat olive oil and brown livers on both sides. Add chicken stock, lemon juice and remaining ingredients. Reduce until sauce thickens. If livers are not completely cooked (no blood), add 2 oz of water or chicken stock and continue to reduce. Salt and pepper are key to the success of this recipe. Serve with rigatoni.

Serves 4 to 6

CARBONARA

Friends will flock to your kitchen from the incredible aroma of carbonara.

1 1/3 cups chopped raw bacon or prosciutto
1 small onion (chopped thin)
5 oz Parmesan cheese
3 cloves minced garlic
3 whole eggs (whisk in small bowl)
salt & pepper to taste
1 oz olive oil
3 oz chicken stock or water

In a heated pan add olive oil, bacon and onion. Brown thoroughly. Drain excess oil from pan. Prepare your pasta, drain and transfer to large mixing bowl. Cover to keep hot. In the same pan heat bacon, onion, garlic, salt & pepper, and chicken stock. Reduce by 1/2. Pour over pasta and add egg mixture and cheese. Carefully toss and serve. Rigatoni or farfalle is a perfect pasta choice. Garnish with cracked black pepper.

Serves 4 to 6

HERB'S FLORENTINE

This recipe has been passed on through Sue's family for the past 15 years. Please enjoy our version.

1/2 lb chopped bacon
2 onions (chopped)
2 eggs (whipped)
10 oz chopped spinach
8 oz chicken stock or water
1 oz olive oil
pinch dried basil
4 oz Parmesan cheese
1 green pepper (chopped)
1 red pepper (chopped)
1/2 lb mushrooms (sliced)
4 cloves garlic (minced)
1/4 teaspoon cayenne
1/2 teaspoon allspice
pinch dried oregano
salt & pepper to taste

In a pan heat olive oil and cook bacon, onions, peppers and mushrooms. When thoroughly cooked add stock and seasonings. Reduce. In a large mixing bowl toss pasta (we suggest spaghetti) with egg, sauce and cheese. Serve with cracked black pepper and shaved Parmesan.

Serves 6 to 8

LASAGNA

PORTABELLA MUSHROOM LASAGNA

This Cucina Bella favorite is so popular that customers reserve slices with their reservations. We are very humbled by this and hope you will enjoy our house specialty lasagna.

3 1/2 lb portabella mushrooms (stems removed & chopped fine, caps sliced 1/4 inch thick)
1 white onion (diced thin)
1 oz olive oil
1 oz lemon juice
3 oz flour
2 lb spinach
1 1/2 lb grated provolone
1 lb Ricotta cheese
1/2 lb grated Parmesan cheese
20 oz lasagna noodles (uncooked)
3 oz unsalted butter
2 1/2 qt heavy whipping cream

In a large pan heat olive oil and slowly cook onions. Add mushroom stems and cook on low heat for 45 minutes. Remove mixture to food processor, grind and set aside. Using the same pan, cook mushroom caps until tender (4 to 5 minutes). Set aside for later lasagna assembly. Using a heavy pot, reduce lemon juice by 1/2. Add butter and flour to make a light mix. Add heavy cream, reduce heat, stir occasionally until juice has dissolved. Add ground mixture and cook for 45 minutes on low heat. Salt and pepper to taste.

To assemble Portabella Mushroom Lasagna: In a lasagna pan or deep baking pan layer bottom with raw lasagna noodles. Place spinach, cheeses, mushroom caps and sauce in layers. Continue this process, remembering to save cheeses for top. Cover with aluminum foil. Bake for 45 minutes at 450 degrees. Remove aluminum foil and brown cheese on top for ten minutes. Slice and serve hot.

Serves 8 to 10

GREEN TOMATO LASAGNA

At the end of the summer, Grandma Koger always sends us bags of green tomatoes from her prolific garden in St. John, Indiana. We use the tomatoes for decoration in the restaurant (where they actually ripen) and even fry them up for a great appetizer special. Out of sheer desperation to use up the scuds of green tomatoes, we created this incredible and popular summer recipe.

3 to 4 lb firm green tomatoes (sliced thin)
1 egg
16 oz provolone (grated)
8 oz grated parmesan
1 tablespoon dried basil
1 box dried lasagna noodles (raw, do not cook)
16 oz Ricotta cheese
3 quarts Panna sauce
1 tablespoon dried oregano

In a medium bowl combine Ricotta, provolone, Parmesan, egg, basil and oregano (cheese mixture). In a 9x13 lasagna pan spread 1 cup Panna sauce, layer of noodles, layer of green tomatoes and a layer of cheese mixture. Repeat procedure. End with noodles and top with cheese. Pour excess Panna sauce over the top. Cover with aluminum foil. Bake at 375 degrees for 45 minutes, uncover and brown for 15 minutes more. Partially cool, slice and serve.

Serves 8 to 10

VEGETABLE LASAGNA

The traditional and authentic approach of using uncooked lasagna noodles saves time and creates a sturdier lasagna.

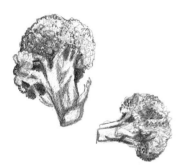

VEGETABLE FILLING
1 1/2 cups onion (chopped)
4 cloves garlic (minced)
1/2 lb chopped mushrooms
3 tablespoons sherry
1 tablespoon olive oil
2 cups chopped broccoli
10 oz spinach
1/2 teaspoon salt
1 cup zucchini (sliced)
pinch dried oregano & basil

CHEESE MIXTURE
16 oz Ricotta cheese
8 oz grated mozzarella
1/2 cup grated Parmesan
1/4 cup Italian parsley (chopped)
2 eggs

NOODLES AND SAUCE
20 oz lasagna noodles (uncooked)
25 oz Cucina Bella Marinara

In a large pan sauté vegetable filling. Broccoli should be tender. In a medium mixing bowl combine cheese mixture. In a lasagna pan or deep baking pan spread a cup of sauce, layer with lasagna noodles (uncooked), vegetable filling then cheese filling. Repeat process; finish with noodles and top with sauce. Sprinkle with grated Parmesan cheese. Cover with aluminum foil and bake at 375 degrees for 30 minutes. Remove foil and brown for 10 minutes. Cut and serve hot.

Serves 8 to 10

CHICKEN CACCIATORE
(Chicken the Hunter's Way)

Hearty stews and casseroles have proved to be a staple at Cucina Bella. Here's our favorite.

3 tablespoons olive oil
4 oz mushrooms (halved)
2 lb chicken pieces
2 cloves garlic (chopped)
1/2 white onion (chopped)
1 cup chicken stock
16 oz Cucina Bella Marinara
1 teaspoon oregano
1 tablespoon fresh rosemary
2 oz black pitted olives
2 tablespoons chopped parsley
salt & pepper to taste
2 oz grated Parmesan cheese

In a large pan add olive oil and pre-cook mushrooms, onions and olives. Remove from oil and put into ovenproof casserole. In a frying pan brown chicken pieces and put into same oven-proof casserole. Preheat oven at 350 degrees. In casserole add remaining ingredients. Bake at 350 degrees for 45 minutes to an hour. Finish by sprinkling with grated Parmesan cheese.

Serves 6 to 8

EGGPLANT PARMESAN

This vegetarian delight proves as hearty as the more traditional chicken dish.

1 large eggplant
1 cup olive oil
8 oz Cucina Bella Marinara
3 tablespoons grated Parmesan cheese
6 oz mozzarella cheese (sliced thin)
1/4 cup chopped fresh basil
salt & pepper to taste

Peel eggplant and cut into thin slices. Salt and pepper each slice. Fry in oil until brown and drain well on paper towel or kitchen towel. Place 1/2 of the eggplant in ovenproof casserole and add sauce, Parmesan and a layer of mozzarella. Repeat procedure with remaining 1/2 eggplant, sauces and cheeses. Bake at 400 degrees for 20 minutes. Sprinkle with grated Parmesan and chopped basil. Serve hot.

Serves 4 to 6

FRIENDSHIP CHICKEN

We love this hearty recipe, which we have refined over the past two years. Friendship Chicken is a favorite closing entree for our kitchen table, as well as a popular daily chef's specialty.

1 red pepper (cleaned & diced)
1 yellow pepper (cleaned & diced)
1 small onion (diced)
2 garlic cloves (diced)
2 tablespoons olive oil
2 1/2 pounds chicken pieces (brown in olive oil 5 minutes on each side)
1/4 cup red wine
2 plum tomatoes (quartered)
salt & pepper to taste
1/2 cup water
1/2 cup chicken stock
8 black olives (pitted)
1/4 teaspoon chopped oregano
1 tablespoon chopped Italian parsley
1 tablespoon mushroom soy (pre-mixed with the 1/2 cup of water)

In a large ovenproof casserole combine all ingredients except red pepper, yellow peppers and tomatoes. Salt and pepper to taste. Place in a 375 degree preheated oven. After 30 minutes add remaining ingredients and cook for an additional 15 to 30 minutes.

Serves 4 to 6

See photograph on page 8

SALTIMBOCCA

This classic Italian favorite remains a non-removable specialty item: 2 years and going strong.

2 pounds veal medallions (pounded very thin and soaked in milk for 24 hours)
1 teaspoon fresh sage
1/4 pound prosciutto
2 tablespoons olive oil
3 tablespoons unsalted butter
salt & pepper to taste
2 tablespoons water
1 tablespoon tomato paste
1/4 cup lemon juice
1 cup flour
1/4 teaspoon dried oregano
1/4 teaspoon dried basil

Combine flour and dried herbs in small mixing bowl. Dredge veal medallions in flour mixture. In a large frying pan on a high flame add olive oil, salt and pepper to taste, fresh sage and prosciutto. Add veal and brown on both sides. Add water, tomato paste and lemon juice. Reduce for 30 seconds. Remove from heat and add butter. Move pan in circular motion until butter is incorporated in sauce. Serve over your favorite pasta. (Turkey can be easily substituted for veal.)

Serves 6

ROULADE
(Rolled Veal With Walnut Stuffing)

Patrons begged us for great veal dishes. We responded with our favorite roulade, which we first enjoyed in Venice.

1 3/4 lb boneless leg of veal
(butterfly & pounded)
4 oz chopped walnuts
4 oz prosciutto
1 oz dried basil
2 oz milk
6 oz fontina cheese
1 oz chopped Italian parsley
2 oz butter (unsalted)
salt & pepper to taste

Arrange prosciutto, fontina, walnuts, parsley and basil on pounded veal. Roll up tight and tie with cooking string. In a medium pan melt butter and brown veal lightly. Add milk, season with salt and pepper to taste and cover. Reduce heat and cook 1 1/2 hours, stirring occasionally until meat has absorbed milk and cooking juices are creamy. Remove string, slice veal roll and serve.

Note: Pounded turkey, pork or chicken can be substituted for veal.

Serves 6

Veal or Pork Piccata

Fast and simple, with an explosion of flavor.

Six 4-oz pork or veal medallions (pounded
    thin and soaked in milk for 24 hours)
6 eggs
2/3 cup Parmesan cheese
salt & pepper to taste
2 oz olive oil
1 cup flour
1 lemon (cut in half)

Veal or pork should be pounded thin with meat mallet, between layers of plastic wrap. Dust each medallion with flour. In a medium mixing bowl whip eggs. Dredge each medallion in egg. Sprinkle with cheese. In a medium pan sauté veal or pork until both sides are brown. Squeeze lemon juice over veal before serving. Serve on your favorite pasta. Salt and pepper are key to the flavor.

Serves 6

CHARLIE'S OXTAILS

This recipe is dedicated to Chef Charlie Socher, who was instrumental during the conception of Cucina Bella. Oh, by the way, Charlie is alive and well and living somewhere in Chicago.

4 lb oxtails
3 tablespoons olive oil
2 slices bacon (diced)
1 onion (sliced)
2 garlic cloves (diced)
1 carrot (diced)
1 teaspoon chopped parsley
1/2 teaspoon salt
1/2 teaspoon pepper
1 1/4 cups dry red wine
3 tablespoons tomato paste
6 celery stalks (cut into 3-inch pieces)

Place oxtails in large pan with olive oil, bacon, onion, garlic, carrot and parsley. Brown both sides of oxtails. Add salt and pepper. Add wine and cook on low heat. When wine evaporates, add tomato paste with enough water to cover oxtails. Cover pan and simmer for 4 1/2 hours. Add celery pieces and cook 15 minutes. Serve over rice or your favorite pasta.

Serves 6 to 8

ROASTED HERBED TURKEY LEGS

Roasted turkey legs along with foccacia stuffing and mushroom gravy are a favorite holiday special as well as our annual Thanksgiving staff dinner.

6 turkey legs
1 oz dried oregano
1 oz dried basil
2 oz olive oil
salt & pepper to taste
4 oz unsalted butter (melted)

In a large oven pan place turkey legs. Sprinkle with olive oil, salt and pepper, basil and oregano. Cover with aluminum foil and bake at 375 degrees for 1 hour. Uncover. Baste with butter and brown for an additional 25 minutes. Serve with Foccacia Stuffing and Mushroom Gravy.

*Note: Save turkey leg drippings for gravy recipe.

Serves 6 to 8

FOCCACIA STUFFING
(Tomato Bread Stuffing)

In a large mixing bowl combine:

9 cups cubed foccacia (dry for 6 hours)
3 tablespoons chopped onion
1/2 cup chopped celery
1/4 cup chopped Italian parsley
season with 1/2 teaspoon salt
2 tablespoons fresh minced sage
1 tablespoons minced rosemary
1 teaspoon fresh minced thyme
12 oz chicken stock
2 tablespoons melted butter

Combine all ingredients and mix well. Transfer to 9 x 13-inch buttered baking pan and bake at 350 degrees for 20 to 30 minutes.

*Note: Foccacia bread can be purchased at any Italian specialty store.

Serves 6 to 8

MUSHROOM GRAVY

3 tablespoons turkey drippings
1 tablespoon butter
2 tablespoons flour
1/4 pound sliced button mushrooms
1 teaspoon mushroom soy sauce
1/4 cup red wine
2 cups cool water or chicken stock

In a medium sauce pan add 3 tablespoons turkey drippings, butter and 2 tablespoons flour. Whisk over low heat until smooth. Add 1/4 pound sliced button mushrooms, 1 teaspoon mushroom soy sauce and 1/4 cup red wine. Stir constantly. Reduce by 1/2 and add 2 cups cool water or chicken stock. Heat until gravy is thick.

Serves 6 to 8

SEAFOOD STEW

*Served in a hollowed-
out loaf of crusty
Italian bread, this
will impress at every
dinner party.*

16 oz white fish (cut into 1-inch cubes)
1 onion (chopped)
1 oz olive oil
3 cloves garlic (minced)
12 oz tomato sauce
6 oz dry white wine
2 tablespoons each: basil, thyme and oregano
1 bay leaf
2 tablespoons chopped Italian parsley
4 oz frozen corn
4 oz frozen peas
8 oz shrimp (cleaned & deveined)
8 oz mussels
8 oz scallops
8 oz calamari (cut into rings)

In a large pot heat olive oil and cook onions
and garlic. Add tomato sauce, corn, peas, wine
and seasonings. Simmer 25 minutes, stirring
occasionally. Add mussels. When mussels begin to
open, add remaining seafood. Cook for 3 minutes.
Add fresh parsley.

Serves 6 to 8

New Zealand Green Lipped Mussels With Orange

32 oz mussels (fresh, unopened)
4 oz dry white wine
2 oranges (cut in half)
1 oz chopped parsley
2 oz olive oil
salt & pepper to taste

In a large pot preheat olive oil. Add mussels, wine, salt and pepper. Squeeze the juice of the oranges and add parsley. Cover and cook for 5 minutes. All shells should be opened. Remove mussels. Reduce sauce on high flame until sauce thickens by half and pour over mussels. Bread for sopping is an absolute must.

Serves 6 to 8

Braised Beef With Onions and Carrots

Many private parties and catering events have enjoyed this Cucina Bella specialty.

1/4 lb slab bacon (blanch in hot water
   for 5 minutes, then cut into cubes)
2 1/2 to 3 lb beef brisket
6 allspice berries
6 onions (thinly sliced)
1 teaspoon salt
1/2 teaspoon black pepper
8 carrots peeled (cut into 2-inch pieces)
1 cup water
1 cup butter

Preheat oven to 350 degrees. Insert bacon cubes into brisket by making small, random cuts. Do the same with the allspice. Line the bottom of a roasting pan with the onions, carrots and leftover bacon. Sprinkle brisket with salt and pepper. Cover tightly and bake 4 hours. Turn the brisket every 30 to 45 minutes. Add butter and water for the last 20 minutes. Slice and serve.

Serves 6 to 8

TUSCAN POT PIE

PASTRY DOUGH
2 cups flour
1/2 teaspoon baking power
1 teaspoon salt
1 cup unsalted butter
1/4 cup ice water

Combine all dry ingredients in mixing bowl. Cut butter into flour mixture until it resembles fine crumbs. Add water and knead the dough until it is workable and pliable. Let the dough sit covered for 30 minutes. Sprinkle flour on work surface and rolling pin; roll out dough to desired size, keeping in mind that you want to cover the size of your 9-inch casserole dish. Place the flattened dough on baking sheet pan and chill.

FILLING
8 - 10 oz sweet Italian sausage (precooked)
2 potatoes (diced)
2 carrots (diced)
1 zucchini (diced)
1 onion (diced)
1 tablespoon olive oil
2 cups heavy whipping cream
1/2 cup tomato paste
1/2 teaspoon oregano
1/2 teaspoon basil
salt & pepper to taste

In a small mixing bowl combine cream, tomato paste and dried herbs; set aside. In a large frying pan, over a high flame, add olive oil, potatoes, carrots, zucchini and onion; cook until brown. Then add sausage and cream mixture. Salt and pepper to taste. Pour ingredients into a large casserole dish. Cover top of casserole with pastry and seal all edges. Punch a 1/2-inch hole in center of pastry. Bake at 350 degrees for 17-22 minutes, until crust is golden brown. Allow to set for a few minutes before serving.

Serves 6 to 8

POT ROAST OF BEEF

We introduced this hearty recipe to help cure the winter blahs and reinforce the warmth provided by Italian comfort foods.

5 lb beef rump or chuck
1/4 cup red wine
salt & ground pepper
3 tablespoons dried basil
1 bay leaf
4 plum tomatoes quartered
1 tablespoon lemon juice
8 garlic cloves (minced)
3 leeks (diced)
5 whole carrots (sliced)
3 large onions each stuck with two cloves
3 cups beef broth or water
6 potatoes (sliced)
6 oz tomato paste

Season meat with salt, ground pepper and dried basil. Preheat oven at 375 degrees. In a large pot or large ovenproof casserole place beef, garlic, basil, leeks, carrots, potatoes, onions, bay leaf and beef broth. Bake in oven for one hour covered. Uncover and add tomatoes, tomato paste, lemon juice and red wine. Cover and cook over low flame on stovetop for 1 1/2 to 2 hours. Baste every 30 minutes. Slice and serve.

Serves 6 to 8

STUFFED SHELLS

This stuffed shells recipe has been passed down for years in Sue's family. Here is our very popular version, one of Sue's favorites.

1/2 box jumbo shells cooked according to package directions (drain in cold water and set aside)

In Mixing Bowl Combine:

15 oz Ricotta cheese
2 tablespoons diced sun-dried tomatoes
25 fresh basil leaves (whole)
1 egg
salt & pepper to taste
Cucina Bella Marinara to cover

Stuff shells with combined cheese mixture. Preheat oven at 350 degrees. In a 9x13-inch baking pan put 3 cups Cucina Bella Marinara. Place stuffed shells on top of sauce. Cover with aluminum foil and bake for 20 minutes. Remove cover and bake an additional 10 minutes.

Serves 6 to 8

GELATO

CUCINA BELLA ICE CREAM

(Gelato Cucina Bella)

The progression and initial intervention of Cucina Bella Gelato was a very rewarding and successful venture. During 2 1/2 weeks of testing and experimentation, we discovered and literally created our own unique style of ice cream making that translates perfectly to the Cucina Bella Cookbook. These recipes are so accessible and simple that we even shocked ourselves. Originally we were making gelatos daily, almost to order, and serving them out of our ice cream maker, literally, with giant spoons and frozen wooden bowls. Servers went on sales rampages, demand quadrupled, and we were sent into ice cream "hell" trying to figure out a method that met the demands of a full 80-seat dining room, a 40-seat outdoor street café, a 10-seat Kitchen Table, 6-seat Chef's Table and a 12-seat Chef's Herb Garden. The following are our original recipes; nothing like these has ever been in print. They are our surefire winners and solved our enormous task of providing gelato to the masses of Chicago's Lincoln Park.

We have separated our recipes into two types, A and B. Type A is a basic vanilla with 1 major ingredient, and Type B is a basic chocolate. You will need a medium mixing bowl and a food processor. "86" your commercial ice cream maker (I know I will certainly hear about this), and any cooking on the stove is also "86'ed".

SPECIAL NOTE TO REMEMBER FOR GELATO MAKING:

Taste your initial creation after blending in food processor. You may want to increase the fruit, sugar or special flavoring. You may also want to decrease ingredients for the future.

Once you have mastered our simple approach, you can become creative and design your own recipes, following the standard amounts given. New combinations and ingredient substitution may create a real winner that you can be proud of making. A light dusting of confectioners' sugar or cocoa powder (when appropriate) adds the perfect finale to the suggested garnishes.

These recipes are to be frozen for 24 hours and served within 48 hours. Excessive freezing causes the composition to deteriorate slightly.

Cucina Bella Ice Cream

Type A Standard Vanilla Gelato

In a medium mixing bowl combine:

4 cups heavy whipping cream

2 eggs

1/2 cup sugar

2 teaspoons vanilla extract

2 pinches salt

Type B Standard Chocolate Gelato

4 cups heavy whipping cream

4 eggs

3/4 cup sugar

2 teaspoons vanilla extract

2 pinches salt

1 cup cocoa powder

3 oz cream de cocoa liqueur

1 cup brewed espresso

Mix ingredients, by hand, until thoroughly combined. Transfer mixture to food processor and blend until consistency reaches that of a creamy milkshake or thick mousse. Pour mixture into a plastic container with lid. For crunchy, chunky or nonprocessed ingredients (*e.g.*, blueberries, pecans), add on top of mixture and stir in with spatula 2 times. Freeze for 8 to 12 hours. Remove from freezer 15 minutes prior to serving. Gelato is ready to serve.

Serves 6 to 8

MINTED CHOCOLATE STRAWBERRY

FOLLOW RECIPE B

Add 2 eggs
4 oz liqueur (white chocolate)
1/2 cup sugar
2 oz lemon juice
3 oz fresh mint (no stems)
20 oz fresh strawberries
1 oz mint schnapps

Garnish with fresh mint, shaved white and dark chocolate and sliced strawberries.

CHOCOLATE RASPBERRY GELATO

FOLLOW RECIPE B

Add 2 eggs
3 oz raspberry liqueur
20 oz fresh raspberries

Garnish with fresh raspberries or a shot of raspberry liqueur.

CHOCOLATE CAPPUCCINO GELATO

FOLLOW RECIPE B

Add 2 eggs
2 cups brewed espresso
4 oz chocolate liqueur
1 oz ground espresso beans
1/2 cup sugar

Garnish with whipped cream, ground espresso and whole coffee beans (3 to 4). A dash of chocolate liqueur on top is a perfect finish.

BLACKBERRY PINE NUT GELATO

FOLLOW RECIPE A

Add 2 eggs
pinch of salt
dash of almond extract
1 oz lemon juice
3 oz blackberry liqueur
1 cup toasted pine nuts (bake or sauté
   for 1 minute)
pinch of nutmeg
20 oz fresh blackberries

Garnish with fresh blackberries, mint and toasted pine nuts.

BLUEBERRY GELATO

FOLLOW RECIPE A

Add 1 egg
3 oz blueberry liqueur (optional)
2 oz lemon juice
20 oz fresh blueberries

Garnish with fresh blueberries or a shot of blueberry liqueur.

STRAWBERRY GELATO

FOLLOW RECIPE A

Add 1 egg
3 oz strawberry liqueur (optional)
2 oz lemon juice
20 oz fresh strawberries

Garnish with fresh strawberries or a shot of strawberry liqueur.

HAZELNUT VANILLA GELATO

FOLLOW RECIPE A

1 teaspoon vanilla extract
3 oz hazelnut liqueur
1 egg
1 cup toasted walnuts and rosemary (add 1/2 oz olive oil to walnuts and one sprig rosemary [no stem]; bake or sauté for 1 minute)

Garnish with shot of hazelnut liqueur and toasted rosemary walnuts.

PEAR MANGO MINT GELATO

FOLLOW RECIPE A

3 oz pear liqueur
4 cored and skinned pears
2 cored and skinned mangoes
2 oz fresh mint (no stems)

Garnish with slice of pear and sprig of mint.

DESSERTS

GRANDMA NONNI MINAUDO'S BREAD PUDDING

The bread pudding of Cucina Bella is hands down the most popular and most requested recipe. Chef Charlie Socher was instrumental in its progression. Please enjoy.

3 oz sugar
1 1/2 tablespoons almond liqueur
3 eggs
6 oz buttermilk
dash of cinnamon
8 oz heavy cream (scalded)
1/8 loaf Italian bread (cubed, no crust)

Mix sugar, eggs, almond liqueur, buttermilk and dash of cinnamon in a large mixing bowl. Add heavy cream and bread cubes. Carefully portion Five 4-oz servings into small bowls. Place in water bath and bake at 350 degrees for 22 - 25 minutes. Garnish with caramel or bourbon sauce. Finish with fresh fruit, mint and confectioners' sugar garnish.

Serves 5 individuals or makes 1 large serving

GRAPE FLAN

3 tablespoons flour
8 tablespoons sugar
18 oz milk
2 egg yolks
zest of 1/2 lemon
1 large bunch grapes (for garnish)

In small pot heat ingredients, whisking gently until thick. Pour into 4 small bowls and cool. When cool, top with fresh seedless grapes. Garnish with fresh mint and grape leaf and sprinkle with confectioners' sugar.

Serves 4

CROSTADA

(Banana Caramel Walnut Tart)

We produce crostadas on a daily basis at Cucina Bella. The many different combinations are beautiful. Here's our favorite.

2 cups flour
1/2 teaspoon baking powder
1 teaspoon salt
1 cup unsalted butter
1/4 cup ice water
1/2 cup sugar & sugar for sprinkling
2 cups diced bananas
1/2 chopped walnuts

Combine all dry ingredients in medium mixing bowl. Cut butter into flour mixture until it resembles fine crumbs. Add water and knead the dough until it is workable and pliable. Let the dough sit covered for 30 minutes. Sprinkle flour on work surface and rolling pin; roll out dough. Using a five-inch plate cut out 6 crostada circles. Place on a buttered cookie sheet. Sprinkle with sugar. In the middle of each crostada fill centers of pastry dough with bananas and walnuts. Crimp edges so dough leans toward middle of crostada. Bake at 375 degrees for 15 to 17 minutes. Serve hot. Drizzle with homemade caramel. Garnish with fresh fruit (we prefer strawberries) and mint leaves.

Serves 6

BLUEBERRY COFFEE ICE

Homemade granitas are one of the classical favorites from Cucina Bella's extensive dessert list. The combination of blueberries and coffee makes a perfect dessert on a summer evening in our outdoor café. This recipe gives coffee lovers a cure for their sweet tooth while refreshing their taste buds with the flavor of fresh blueberries.

1 1/2 cups water
4 oz brewed espresso
1/2 cup chilled whipping cream
mint leaves for garnish
1 cup sugar
1 cup fresh blueberries
   (ground in food processor)
1 tablespoon lemon juice

In a heavy medium saucepan combine water and sugar over medium heat until sugar dissolves and syrup boils for 3 minutes. Cool syrup. Mix in coffee, blueberries and lemon juice. Pour mixture into medium-size mixing bowl. Freeze until mixture is solid. Using a fork or large spoon, scrape mixture to form flakes. Break up all chunks. Return to freezer. Keep frozen until ready to serve. Scoop granitas into coffee cup, "trendy" cappuccino cup or elegant stemware. Top with whipped cream and garnish with fresh mint. Lightly sprinkle with ground espresso coffee beans.

Serves 4 to 6 servings

PEACH ICE

1 1/2 lb peaches (peeled, stones removed)
1 oz lemon juice
5 1/2 oz sugar
5 oz water

Place peaches and lemon juice in a food processor
and puree. Dissolve sugar and water in small pan.
Cook for 4 - 16 minutes until thick. Set to cool.
When cool, mix with peaches and freeze. Take out
of freezer and whisk 2 or 3 times at 15-minute
intervals to achieve a smooth and crystal-free
texture. Garnish with fresh mint.

LEMON ORANGE ICE

2 cups warm water
3/4 cups sugar
1/2 cup orange juice
1/2 cup lemon juice
zest of 1 orange

In a mixing bowl melt sugar in warm water. Add
orange zest, orange juice and lemon juice. Freeze.
Scrape mixture to form flakes. Break up all
chunks. Garnish with orange slice.

FLOURLESS CHOCOLATE ESPRESSO CAKE

8 oz semisweet chocolate
8 oz sugar
8 oz butter (unsalted)
1 double espresso
5 eggs (beaten)

Melt chocolate, sugar and butter over double boiler, add espresso. Beat eggs and add to the chocolate mixture. Wrap a 9-inch greased spring-form pan in foil. This will keep the cake mix from leaking out. Pour cake mixture into pan and cover tightly with foil. Place cake in warm water bath and bake (poach) at 350 degrees for 65 minutes. Serve with shaved chocolate garnish or blueberry sauce.

Serves 4 to 6

CHOCOLATE ESPRESSO MOUSSE

18 oz chocolate
9 egg yolks
4 tablespoons sugar
24 oz heavy whipping cream
1 double espresso

Melt chocolate over double boiler. In a separate mixing bowl beat eggs and sugar. Add espresso and egg mixture to melted chocolate and mix. Easily fold in heavy whipping cream, which you have whipped to stiff peaks in a separate bowl. Refrigerate for 2 hours. Serve in large stemware.

Serves 8 to 10

LEANING TOWER OF PISA

Pizzelles are an ancient, traditional Italian thin cookie and are available at most markets or specialty stores. In a pastry bag with a large tip, fill bag with chocolate mousse. On a plate, squeeze a dollop of mousse and stack a pizzelle. Continue this process 6 pizzelles high. Garnish with shaved chocolate, confectioners' sugar and fruit. Carefully lean stack. The Leaning Tower of Pisa will dazzle at any dinner party. The tower is our top-selling dessert.

One tower easily serves 2

125

BAKED APPLES LICATA

This recipe will prove to be a perfect and easy finish to any dinner party, casual or formal.

8 apples
1 cup raisins
1/4 cup white wine
1/4 teaspoon cinnamon
1/4 teaspoon grated lemon rind
4 tablespoons sugar
1 1/2 tablespoons butter (unsalted)

Core apples. Soak raisins in white wine for 45 minutes. Stuff centers of apples with raisins, and sprinkle with lemon rind and sugar. Dot with butter and sprinkle with wine from raisin marinade. Bake 45 minutes at 375 degrees. Serve hot or cold. Garnish with dashes of cinnamon and confectioners' sugar.

Serves 8

CANNOLI

1 1/3 cups flour
1 tablespoon shortening
pinch of salt
1/2 teaspoon sugar
white wine (sweet or dry)

In a medium mixing bowl, mix ingredients and add just enough wine to make a stiff but workable dough. Roll into ball and let stand for 1 hour. Roll out dough 1/8 inch thick and cut into 5-inch squares. Place cannoli tube across the corners of the square. Fold one corner around the tube, then the other and mesh together. Fry one at a time until golden brown. Remove cannoli and let cool before filling.

*Note: cannoli tubes can be purchased at Italian specialty stores.

CANNOLI RICOTTA FILLING

1 pound Ricotta (strain excess liquid)
2 tablespoons confectioners' sugar
2 tablespoons chocolate chips
1 tablespoon orange peel or orange marmalade
1 jigger cream de cocoa or orange liqueur

Using a hand mixer, cream mixture well. Fill shells with Ricotta filling. Garnish with chocolate chips, fruit, nuts and confectioners' sugar.

Serves 12

LEMON PINE NUT BISCUITS

We use these delicious biscuits as garnish for our espressos and cappuccinos.

1 1/2 cups sugar
4 eggs
1/4 teaspoon grated lemon rind
2 teaspoons lemon juice
2 cups pastry flour
2 tablespoons confectioners' sugar
3 tablespoons pine nuts

In a double boiler beat eggs and sugar in a small mixing bowl until mixture is lukewarm. Remove from hot water. Continue beating until mixture is foaming and cool. Add lemon juice, lemon rind and flour and fold gently. On buttered and floured large cookie sheets drop teaspoonfuls of batter 1 inch apart. Sprinkle with confectioners' sugar and pine nuts. Let stand for 10 minutes and bake at 375 degrees for 15 - 17 minutes.

Yields approximately 40 cookies

STUFFED PEACHES LATINO

6 large ripe peaches
1/4 lb ground amaretti biscuits
3 tablespoons almond liqueur
2 egg yolks
9 tablespoons sugar
1/3 cup chopped almonds
1/4 cup butter (unsalted)
chopped peach flesh (instructions below)

Preheat oven at 350 degrees. Cut peaches in half and remove stones. Using a spoon, remove some peach flesh from the centers of the peach halves; save flesh. In a mixing bowl combine remaining ingredients. Mix thoroughly and stuff individual peach halves. On an oiled baking pan place peach halves; top with a pat of butter. Bake for 32 minutes. Sprinkle with confectioners' sugar and garnish with amaretti biscuits and fresh mint.

Serves 6 to 8

CUCINA COCONUT CAKE

Coconut lovers rave about this simple but tasty dessert. Berry sauce is a perfect accompaniment.

1 1/2 cups flour
3/4 cup fine granulated sugar
4 teaspoons baking powder
1 egg
1/2 cup milk
6 tablespoons melted butter
1/2 lemon rind (finely diced)
2/3 cup grated coconut
confectioners' sugar (for dusting)

Preheat oven to 350 degrees. In a medium mixing bowl combine flour, baking powder and sugar. In a separate bowl beat egg, milk and melted butter and then place inside the center of the flour mixture. Add coconut and lemon rind. Beat well until a thick batter occurs. Pour in 8-inch pre-buttered cake pan. Cook for 37 minutes. Cake should be crisp and golden. Cool; sprinkle with confectioners' sugar and grated coconut.

Serves 6 to 8

CHOCOLATE-COVERED SEEDLESS GRAPES

We discovered this very popular dessert during our travels in Italy. A street vendor was selling them along with many other chocolate-covered fruits. This authentic dessert still remains one of the most popular and most original here at Cucina Bella.

In a double boiler melt 6 oz of chocolate. When chocolate is melted, dip one large bunch of grapes. Gently shake off excess chocolate. Let the grapes sit for 30 minutes to dry. In a double boiler melt 1 oz of white chocolate. With a fork, drizzle white chocolate over the bunch of grapes. Pears, apricots, and strawberries are also an incredible alternative.

Serves 2

DESSERT SAUCES

BLUEBERRY SAUCE

12 oz sugar
12 oz blueberries (fresh or frozen)
1/2 oz lemon juice

Place all ingredients in a small heavy pot and
reduce on high heat for 10 minutes. Strain sauce.
Serve hot or cold.

Follow same steps for a raspberry sauce,
blackberry sauce or combination berry sauce
(4 oz of each).

CHOCOLATE GANACHE

3 3/4 cups sweet chocolate
1 tablespoon light corn syrup
1/4 cup milk
1 1/2 cups heavy whipping cream

Chop chocolate into small pieces and combine
with corn syrup in mixing bowl. Heat cream and
milk and add to chocolate and syrup. Mix until
melted. Keep warm. Use as frosting for your
favorite cake, torte or specialty dessert. Great
for dipping fresh fruit.

HOMEMADE CARAMEL

16 oz sugar
1 oz lemon juice
1 oz water
8 oz heavy whipping cream

On medium heat in a large pan slowly cook sugar and lemon juice. Use a wooden spoon to stir and chop constantly. Add water. In 10-15 minutes sugar will begin to brown. A rich caramel color will appear, and the aroma is unmistakable. Remove from heat and slowly stir in cream. Stir vigorously. Return to heat and bring to boil. Serve hot or cold.

CAPPUCCINO CARAMEL

Simply add 1 oz espresso to your 8 oz heavy whipping cream.

BOURBON SAUCE

1/2 lb butter (soft)
1 cup sugar
1 cup brown sugar
8 oz white corn syrup
1/3 cup water
2 whipped eggs
1 teaspoon vanilla
3/4 cup bourbon

In a mixing bowl combine butter, corn syrup, sugars and water. Heat to 175 degrees. Add eggs, vanilla and bourbon. Cook, stirring constantly, for 6 - 10 minutes. Serve hot or cold.

Chocolate-Covered Pear, page 131

DOG AND CAT COOKIES

The popularity of our summer outdoor doggie dining still astounds us and warms our hearts.

1 large beet with greens on
1/2 cup nonfat dry milk
1 cup wheat germ

Boil beet in water until tender. Drain beet and puree in food processor. Add milk and wheat germ and mix. Shape into 1/2-inch balls and bake on cookie sheet at 350 degrees for 15 - 20 minutes or until golden brown.

INDEX

GLOSSARY

al dente	undercooked, point before pasta is fully cooked
baste	reapply liquid, cover with broth or stock
blanch	precook in boiling water for 30 - 45 seconds
brisket	a specific cut of meat, from the chest region
brush	lightly cover with liquid, use pastry brush
charred	thoroughly cooked on grill, almost black
crimp	pinch, seal
core	remove core, seeds
crumbled	broken by hand into smaller pieces
deglaze	use a liquid to pull cooked flavors from a hot pan
detached	pulled apart, detach stem
deveined	dark vein removed through small cut on top of shrimp
dice	cut into small, even square pieces
dollop	a small amount, size of silver dollar
dot	a very small amount, size of pea
double boiler	a piece of kitchen hardware with one pan over another that contains boiling water
drained	all liquid removed
dredge	thoroughly cover with some force
drippings	liquid from meats and poultry after cooking
flesh	reference to main substance of product, pulp
fold	gently combine with spatula
finish	add a final touch, last
flip	toss or mix garnish for presentation
fry	pan fry, cook in pan
garnish	decorate

glaze	lightly cover
grate	use grater to break into smaller pieces
high flame	full strength, high power
marinate	soak in flavored liquids
meat	reference to main substance of product, pulp
mesh	connect, bond or become one
minced	finely chopped by hand
pinch	a small amount, least amount of ingredient
poach	cook in water or other liquid
precooked	prepared in advance
puree	combine or mince in food processor
raw	uncooked
reduce	cook liquid from one consistency to thicker or less-dense consistency
sauce hard	high flame to rolling boil
roux	thickener, combination of flour and butter
rub	use hands to lightly coat
rolling boil	full-out boil at boiling point
simmer	cook on a low heat
shaved	sliced thin
soak	marinate, store in liquid
sop	use bread to soak up remaining sauce so it can be eaten
sprinkle	lightly cover with finesse
stone	seed of fruit
strain	use a wire mesh to remove seeds or pulp
tie	wrap and secure with cooking string waterbath cooking in water
whip	use a whisk to mix, soft or hard
whisk	a piece of kitchen hardware used to whip food
86'ed	does not exist, all gone, bah-bye